# Monotonies of the Wildlife

*poems by*

# William Erickson

*Finishing Line Press*
Georgetown, Kentucky

# Monotonies of the Wildlife

Copyright © 2022 by William Erickson
ISBN 978-1-64662-677-9 First Edition
All rights reserved under International and Pan-American Copyright Conventions. No part of this book may be reproduced in any manner whatsoever without written permission from the publisher, except in the case of brief quotations embodied in critical articles and reviews.

## ACKNOWLEDGMENTS

"Player Piano" was shortlisted by the UK journal *Wildfire Words* and appears in their *Transformations Anthology*.

To my mother, whose support knows no limit. To my father, for experience, stories, and perspective. To my wife, for more patience than one ought to afford anyone. Especially to my mentor, friend, and teacher Dr. Desiree Hellegers. Your constant encouragement is the gravity that pulled these poems from an illegible notebook into print.

To a robust community of small press poets whose beautiful and diligent work is the rain in my thirsty world. And to the team at Finishing Line Press for their bravery.

These poems are seconds in a lifetime, drops of water falling from branch to branch. In the end they're hardly recognizable.

Publisher: Leah Huete de Maines
Editor: Christen Kincaid
Cover Art: Masen Nichols (Instagram @masen_nichols)
Author Photo: Taylor Jones
Cover Design: Elizabeth Maines McCleavy

Order online: www.finishinglinepress.com
also available on amazon.com

Author inquiries and mail orders:
Finishing Line Press
PO Box 1626
Georgetown, Kentucky 40324
USA

# Table of Contents

## *AS IF SOME WERE SINGING*

Of Self and Morning .................................................................................. 1
Player Piano............................................................................................... 3
Negotiation................................................................................................ 4
Every Rabbit .............................................................................................. 5
In the Cheatgrass ...................................................................................... 6
The Rabbits Who Were Freed .................................................................. 7
Asleep in the Daybed at My Grandmother's............................................ 9
Could've Been Haight Ashbury .............................................................. 10
The Considerate Vermin.......................................................................... 11
The Best Laid Plans ................................................................................ 12
Coins Inside the Anthill .......................................................................... 13
Halfhearted Lighthouse .......................................................................... 14
The order of operations .......................................................................... 15
Montage of the flowers at a cemetery near my home .................... 17
A Pre-Funereal Design ........................................................................... 18
Suspicions in A Common Trail .............................................................. 19
Still life of a parking lot.......................................................................... 20
Outside..................................................................................................... 21
The Birds.................................................................................................. 23

## *THOUGHTS OF A COMMON BITTERNESS*

Tattooed an Afterthought........................................................................ 24
Chapter missing from Revelations ......................................................... 26
Genesis story ........................................................................................... 28
Still life of bible verse ............................................................................ 29
Starting at the fifteenth clause of a preamble to a declaration
    of the liberties of catfish.................................................................... 30
Revelation verse in six lines ................................................................... 31
Neighborhood in several lines................................................................ 32
Interpretation of a modern ideology ...................................................... 33
Don't Reflect a Lot ................................................................................. 34
Catechisms for a Different Day…......................................................... 35

## *AS IF SOME WERE SINGING*

**Of Self and Morning**

Here is an idea, which maybe is something
like myself in parentheses, a grey hair
rumored in my beard, a semicolon
between the days separating cherry
blossoms from topsoil soaking under
clouds as thick as October is.

Here is entropy in ellipses stretching
from something told in dreams,
a bridge for my footprints, and I reply,
as could be expected from one who
clings to railings like they cling to
skin, scars as question marks, sentences
constructed in the lily's fastened blooms,
I reply: Here is the idea of myself, likely
to be proven out by taproots moving earth
aside in search of water, the age-old prayer
of periods like seeds inseminating choices
or directions for the words to go.
Here is the worm in multiples,
the wrinkles near my eyes feeding
principles to silvered glass, as might a robin
gather golden scraps with which
up in branches to build itself a place,
the notion of place and self a mirror
to the puddle where a birdsong
finds its infinite.

Maybe it is myself as leaves in autumn
when the colors burn, maybe fragments,
thought intermittently, with all the order
of untended grass, myself assumed

because today the sun and yesterday
the rain seemed rather genuine,
an idea isolated from the petals
and hyphenated to a change
because the cherry blossoms fall
tomorrow like they did today,

thinking snow before the winter
and before the robin eats.

**Player Piano**

At the edge of a wood a fox
sat with the vibration near him,
interested in the deciduous trees
whose molted disguises burned along
the forest floor. Curious, the vibration
is to be something of a basis upon
which animals, like foxes, hunt or are
hunted, which raises a question as to
the fox's intentions and the
minimal degree of consideration he
affords to the now incontrovertible
tremor climbing up the tree trunks,
causing their naked fingers to dance
against a milk of sky as if playing
keys of an empty piano. One
asks to be seen and the vibration
looks in proportion to the weight
of a body falling to the underbrush,
tinder in the fir and autumn leaves
whose change was meant to hide
the fox. Someday the hunger turns,
and there is a fox whose image
trembles, whose attention to
the vibration suggests he hadn't
thought much further past the leaves
who in the fall have left the forest
floor as warm as his fur.

## Negotiation

Understand today to be that
of the house finch, who in this
early pass pins talons to a
fence slat slightly pulpy still
from afterthoughts of rain
deserting grass outside some
window, perhaps mine. Understand,
too, he's riveted, it seems, to what
may be a fichus on a table making
neither rubber nor figs but pressing
marooned leaves nonetheless
against the glass to scrape away
what sunlight edges in between
the voluptuous bosoms passing
grey and aloof above us. (I say us
only because the house finch and
I catch sight across the double
pane of a certain ambiguity, and
for a spell both watch the fichus
leaves unravel, rather awakened
to a span of time wherein neither
of us could be said to occupy
much else but a branch, and
unclothing themselves naked
to the cold window as if
begging avail of the earliest
inevitabilities of sun.)
And if it isn't entirely unreasonable,
try to think a moment on the strictures
of that occupation, the house finch
clinging to the wood as I to his wary
glance and only in an odd sense
making a sort of conversation
understood to be the day that, between
him and I, is just the same as other days
not expressly his or mine.

**Every Rabbit**

We hung it in an ivy
crawling up between
the weathered slats,
so injured and so torn
from keeping secrets
through the years,
a lucky little rabbit's foot
to catch the sooty rains
as they carved veins across
our shaky fence's weft.

All soaking now, and skeletal,
and fragile bones like feather quills
in off-white habit clinging,
clinging to the woodgrain
for a fortune there
among the leaves in constellation.
How mistaken are the auspices
of children like ourselves—
how simple and deceived.

## In the Cheatgrass

There is an average sense
of salvation in a prairie
across the street, something
which the coyote tastes early
in September, licking at the air
as he might the hunter's blade.
It is the hour of cheatgrass.
A stray word brushing through
suggests an image of the
transaction of pollen and of
rain that speaks a particular
religiosity, an order of importance
germane to our purposes,
which are undecided, which are
categories of breath across a
field imprinting patterns for the
animals to read.

## The Rabbits Who Were Freed

Just across the street from us
a neighbor had a rabbit cage
whose wire walls were
countless little windows.
It set there in the grass
against his fence and watched
in brighter months
the puerile games we'd play,
a pleasant view of things
to no account and of no moment,
unaffected words like breezes
fleeting wastefully.
And as the streetlamps shuddered on
it watched a kindly silence
find the absence of our voices
fine and welcoming.

Sometime near the fall,
before the skies
would grow too cramped
and put in shade
the better parts of shorter days,
the neighbor'd cut a plywood roof
and with some splintered pine
invent the cage a meager refuge
from the weather as it turned.

When winter came he'd hammer nails
in fence posts near the shelter's roof,
at angles pointing upward
where a sky was months before.
Just two or three and none too deep,
so that across the street we'd see
their shadows on the cedar fence
like sundials.

Hours in a rabbit cage.
Hours in a winter.
Hours in the years
we mean to pass.

The neighbor'd always smile and wave
and string a makeshift curtain,
but its ends seemed always loose
enough to see above the rabbit cage
where nails in the fence
would tell the time.
And all those little
windows made from
lattices of wire
must not have ever really freed them
as I thought.

## Asleep in the Daybed at My Grandmother's

When I fall asleep this early in the morning
there's a reoccurring dream I visit
where a walnut tree I used to know
scratches at her roots in the dry,
branny ground beneath a half-hung
moonlight, sometime between the summer
and the fall when there's no season yet
to tell the crows and sparrows how it is.
Her fingertips are frayed and crackle
wildly as she digs, seemingly to
unearth some truth about herself,
or to unearth herself altogether,
not realizing that the deeper down she goes
the weaker and more thirsty she becomes.
And I try hard to stop her digging, but
so small and dumb and naked
I just cut my feet and cry uselessly,
not even able to pick from them
the splinters pushing further as I stand
there underneath her, desperate.
And my blood is rust just like the sky is,
sunless but lucent, turning, but to what,
and if I open my eyes it's Monday
or it's Tuesday, and she just scrapes and etches
while around her crows and sparrows
bob curiously and wait for me to wake.

## Could've Been Haight Ashbury

Saw an ant crossing
the street before the
light had changed,
on her back a bit of
cherry blossom fallen
from a nearby canopy
so mapping her erratic
choices by the pale
rose-blonde touch
of spring she carried.

Aeroplanes and blunt designs
and want of caution cadences,
the blooms of carbon sweetly
tasted waiting for the lights.

Followed her a moment
over the pitted islands
of remaining crosswalk
paint until her clement
path was inscrutable,
and thought perhaps
she was just a perceptual
mistake, a trick of light
against asphalt slickened
over time, and when the
signal changed I walked
indifferent to the thought,
cherry blossom petals
on a breeze littering the
sidewalk behind me for
the next person to sweep.

## The Considerate Vermin

Consider myself to be a copy
of a number of other selves all
vying for the stable pattern of
characteristics peculiar to a field
mouse in running, whose keen
attention the eagle barely works
for propped by an imponderable
thermal, and only for the odd
beauty of an ocean that I won't
be apt to drown within inverting
the strictest contemplation of
a hunt I recognize as but another
sort of breath. A sort of vibration
through the water. And on the
surface I'm a fleeting aggregate
of movements, uncalculated,
an old impulsive dance rehearsed
when I was born and all days since,
and probably now I'm not much
more but blood and habit, my
rather failing eyes aware of a
possibility in an unknown—
diffuse intangibilities—another
breath, a bite of food, and of
the moon another circle. And with
it, replicated, me a hundred thousand
over and I've never really chosen one.
A field mouse in the listing grass
as might be just the same as I.

## The Best Laid Plans

One knelt in the silty ground
near the edge of a small pond,
the other behind him, standing.
In the ripples lapping at its bank
one saw what would be countless
promises, and were it not for a
couple clouds in the sky, one
might've taken for an ocean
the deep expanse of blue repeated
by the shallow water, soft little
breakers like paragraphs of a story
so much bigger than a water of
its size ought to tell. Whisper
in the underbrush.

The rabbit had escaped, but he still
spoke, as such, and the other stood,
wise in that way the moon is
sometimes, with a severity one only
has to trust and not to understand,
and he read pictures on the lake,
not trying much to convince one that
he hadn't a hard obligation soon to
serve. The other believed what
promises he made, but in a different way,
and one had not desire nor capacity
to doubt which ways the other spoke,
but only to close his eyes and hear
the rabbit in the underbrush, the
water filter into sand and over pebbles,
its touch wicking up into the
tired cotton tight around one's knees.

One knelt on the ground and let the
sunshine smile and heard only a
moment what the other said, a
moment gone and every other
moment come the same.

## Coins Inside the Anthill

Here is the hope, or at least
the copy of some sense of hope,
which measured by the pores
it occupies appears to have taken
a liking to the concrete.
Some would say a juxtaposition.
Some would say the texture of
a change, or of a philosophy of
change, which on its face is
an accident the likes of which one
can't explain but can't withhold from
trying,

a poem whose only line is a word
to signify a self, which of itself
refuses to make sense, save, of course,
a sense that to signify itself is its
defining impulse. An ant on the steps
in June when the sun tries harder.

And, if you'll grant a moment of pretense,
a slim and painless moment, really,
but one in which the rust metastasizes
almost imperceptibly, which is of routine
for the likes of things who age by way
of simple duplication, you'll notice that
the footprint of a poem is rather easy
to erase, given that the ants will work.

And, really, that's the hope,
the scores of a footprint
filled back up with soil,
shoots and stems like
splinters so I step as if to
move along.
The age of concrete.

## Halfhearted Lighthouse

But maybe you couldn't have guessed,
white afternoon seen as something
discharged, petals sun-drunk,
with a root slid through the edge
to catch a shadow slip farther down
the shedding clay scrap cliffside.
Suppose a hardly visible trail,
a scar from another time, and
tattooed over since by something
of the unflagging progress of an
undetermined numeral. A retrospective,
which for lack of direction paints the map
in pins to ensure saturation.
Here is a thought, by which a premise
called I am arrives conclusion-wise,
by which the bracketed words are those
with which to build a context—
here is an idea built of constellations
seen too near to city lights,
and by a sort of dyspeptic poetry
mythologized until a self finds
self-inscribed identity to be its meaning.
And you wouldn't have had a clue
but for the heron on the piling,
the one whose unsettled reflection
lays prone as if beneath the weight
of you gazing windswept at her appetence,
a ghost amid the tree-line,
feigned smile and halfhearted lighthouse.

## The order of operations

for a field mouse begins at
the oculus of a den he might
have dug or might have found,
an iris, a type of rotation it
would seem in approaching,
which an hour ago was pitch
but now gains a sort of
translucence, a warmth of
attraction that sets the clock
to its work. If life were a
periscope. Once breaching
the mouse is grass for a
moment in the slight tension,
bending to it now. The blue
is that of repetition swelling
outward and then falling, as
the chest might do in breathing
or the life of trees when seen
in time lapse, and the mouse
is a grain against it, lost but
unaware of it. His chief concern
at present becomes motion,
not as means of travel but as
means of understanding how
the travel asks a question of
him that is difficult. He is a
finger in the dirt scratching
confusedly in a familiar script
we ought to know by now,
something of escape. Don't
the sentences feel nice?

Odd how the grass seems
still at its tips despite the
mouse's pother near the

roots. Supposing his
fundamental aim is left
to be decided by his belly,
the mouse will breathe as
one might to drink

the mountains or the river,
peeling at the layers for a
particular thing to be identified
by hunger and convenience.
Which of an instant might make
one a sort of self-defeatist.
A runner for the urge of it.
But that indeed is the case
of priorities in making, and
what becomes of the field mouse
is more or less the field.

## Montage of the flowers at a cemetery near my home,

Which is the home of
many flowers both in bloom and in an
oxidized state, raindrop-overridden
token gestures omitted as the light
changes, color leaching from petals
into hours.
Into days counted since we saw you last.
Into minutes frozen,
of which skin and latex make confused
the little memories,
of which desaturated
skeletal structures weave a complicated
wreath with which is necklaced
someone's epitaph.
Words and stamens.
Pistils and apologies
as badly worn dialogue
from self to self-repeated,
as might another grieving sentence
pollinate what's left.
Understand it to be rhythmic,
to be the orbital pull of roses to the mud
where red and brown make rusted
places for a love to go.
Understand it to be still life
of the botanist, the author's manuscript
on leaves and stems across the floor
in wait of editing,
to be a reproductive sequence
days and days in making.

Images of hyacinths from seed.
Understand them to be places.
Read them opening and watching.
Read them heavily, as one who
smells the rain and goes out anyhow.
Flashing portraits of the selves
we are in growing old.

**A Pre-Funereal Design**

The people who were ghosts
stood aside watching
the children plant their roses,
an exercise in the quality
of one's speculations and
the prudence of one's fingers,
which is to say experience,
and they asked themselves
in which direction ought the
sprouts to point.
A game of multiples.
And the evening fell as does
the pollen soft and turbid,
as if to add a countless grain
of detail to an emptiness.
Or perhaps it wasn't theirs to say.

## Suspicions in A Common Trail

A friend of mine mentioned
not long before today the
suspiciousness of the cotton
mouse, who after sunlight sifts
the auburn forest floor for where
she thought her home to be, a bit
frantic and disheveled, as it were.
A bit suspicious.
I asked of whom to be suspicious
but one in observation of the day,
which precariously teetering
now finds reason to amend its
understanding of the variegated
hues and broad tonality with which
it took upon to portrait the hours
so far. A matter hitherto decided
and upon which rest, in effect, any
number of dependencies, the likes
of which one cotton mouse at least
seems to be made aware of under
your attention.

## Still life of a parking lot

Untenanted but for the
rabbit and myself, who
recognizing that he hasn't
moved in a moment flushes
red as is the joint above
the rabbit's foot, not quite
rust but nearly, hardened
by July and by the need
to run. Sense of swelling
in the abdomen of both
of us. Sense of impotence
caught up in curiosity
caught up in leaves above
us breaking sun to pieces,
to shadows of the self he'd
been a day ago or more,
stretched across the lawn
some daunting guise
whose remaining foot
perhaps is the auspicious
one. Who finds a question
I won't answer but to turn
and wonder what had
happened, worried but late
for work. See the pupils,
they have patience. They
wait and understand me,
though I haven't done much
except to watch and to wonder
if I'll see the rabbit anymore
today.

## Outside

there is a magnolia
tree whose branches tap
the asbestos siding as if
wanting something of it,
which is assumed to be the
way of trees and houses.
The acceptance of a likeness
made of history and pollen
and myself, or at least a self
who's understanding of the
tree includes a house, perhaps,
which is optimistic, and a little
trite, and the doves are not as
I'd have pictured them once.
Instead they seem as an idea of
the dove I had too long ago to
speak of, as if being told of
them under water and catching
only the inflection of a voice.

Flowers in the summer litter
grass with stamens and pistils
and bring to mind a sentence,
which is taken, as the season is,
to mean something to another
man, but doesn't. And it isn't
different than the dove or the touch
of a magnolia on the siding, is it?
A sort of self in empty spaces where
the branches never reach. A sort
of wisdom in the doves who seem
to know the rain is curious and
wish in coming months to see
the branches where they sleep.

Were I of any difference I'd assume
the trees to be the place in which
I sleep as well, tapping at the siding
of a house in which a man was
sleeping inadvertently,
which is to say I've never known
too much of trees and houses.

## The Birds

I am perhaps concerned
with a sense of today as
one rumored to be cedar
burning. Something loose,
today in a suggestion to run,
which if honesty carries
strikes me as the copy
of an instinct,
the coincidence of leaves
and feathers catching wind
in the same place
for different aims. Funny
how the silence is disquieting,
is today a tautology
of necessity, and of today
a sort of understanding
with the grammar of a thing
who changed, who grew
a memory and a flame
that I can smell again,
that is a sense of smell
its own. And I am anxious
like the bird who smells it
also from the bough I see,
talons deeper in the pith
than what they ought to go
perhaps. Comfort in the grain
splintering, and perhaps a concern
with a sense of today as one
supposed to be behind me
running.

# THOUGHTS OF A COMMON BITTERNESS

**Tattooed an Afterthought**

In a suburb's coffee shop in June,
one of the better days of spring
who want for air and sun and skin
a reacquaintance. Woman,
septuagenarian at least, vinyl capris
from Nike hissing her steps close
to me, stops, and in pseudo-curious
library voice asks do I mind her
looking. Of course not, got them all
for you to peek from safe distance,
blended multi-adjective drink sipping
somewhere closer to the door. As are
mine to read the aging constellations
liver-spotting six-inch stretch of leg
above the coming sock depression.
Take it how you will.
Take for example the question what's
your occupation. Expecting artist, maybe?
Shift at local storeroom closed door broom
push paycheck supporting habits? Hope
they crack the window sometimes.
Listen, needle-skip skin-crawl silence
as I stare her back, "funny how we age
today. Funny the notion of a shadow
following us into evening, into nighttime,
out of place and useless on the floor
as might a skin sloughed away for
want of health and room to breathe
be stubborn to the heal, public toilet
paper tail dragging vestigial evidence
of the shit therein contained."

Beautiful artwork. Love the perspective:
Light up high and rightward, left off

vanishing point so as to avoid looking
very far. Open door to breeze in-rushing,
lovely spring like I remember, like they
used to be, the clouds and the quiet
black crow in the parking lot to pluck
the gravel clean of things to eat.

**Chapter missing from Revelations:**

Oil black Tahoe taking down
asphalt on 33rd again, second,
no, third time in thirty minutes,
twenty-two-inch blade slung
triptych turning three percent
extra on the speedo, so it
just looks fast. Fancy the same
billboard eight-o-eights on shuffle
slow-pass filtered into Sunday
doom-like, bronzed-out Washington
plates to play the treble line. Think
of blacked out power windows
trapping more cacophony, sunlight
trading spots with smoke trails
through the moonroof slipping
after like an anti-turn signal—
showing where it's been, not
where it's going--right hung slow
just like the other two.
In my own garage a turbo
driving tucked eighteens
titanium windpipe aspirated,
loud so that they know the
wastegate's open. Think of
starting early so synthetic
fills the tolerance. Which isn't
even razor thick, which is hairline
spun to keep the needle pinned
despite the same old
speed-trapped freeway drive
to make the interest. Imagine
catalytic tones too deep for
pockets. Picture air diverted
into cylinders, distracted from
a lung somewhere. Stalling
vocal cords in favor of more

ethanol and bass licks.
Think of detour. Think of
easy route to closer finish,
of Escalades in gravel driveways
looping like the mumble rap,
'cause if it's all just run together
what's the difference. Picture
faster finance terms and
slower registration.
Think of detour. Think of
rims or pundits and which
spin I understand to be myself.

**Genesis story:**

737 dressed in UPS gear drilling
clouds above the roof again, screaming,
bag-paper brown and packed.
Suppose the rain is disagreeable.
Picture glass sounds sparkling,
ablated ice etching blight-brown
vinyl wrap as vapor swallows
the Boeing whole, pilots and all.
On the ground, windows tingle.
Murmur through the tresses,
rumor through the studs.
Dirigible seems euphemistic,
which maybe is meta-euphemistic,
which maybe is its purpose.

Offbeat dishes trilling wake the dog,
who in panicked dripping trails
over carpet tail-tucked looking for
the corner, which is found and
burrowed into.
Suppose the cleaner bottle's empty.
Imagine constellations in the shag
by which to navigate an unreasonable
fear of intranational high-speed
shipping soon forgotten.
Air traffic. Flight path morning cigarette.
Imagine moving standard patterns
because the legislature likes
your income, steeper takeoffs so
the sound above the pool might dim
a little sooner.
Imagine breathing thrust,
watching penetration
from the window and parroting
the noise it makes while spoon feeding
someone that you made.

**Still life of bible verse**

Summer morning with grass
cut fresh and honeysuckle bleeding
through a six A.M. window crack,
with primary sounds of starling
origin seasoned by a sprinkling
of in-ground Rain Bird irrigation
whispering the neighbor's income
while it's dusk and no one listens.
Alarm trips memory of grade school
so an instant passes when the thought
of getting up is still improbable,
relief of deliberate wake-up call
so sleeping in is relished. No three
month sabbatical. Forming light makes
warm the kitchen so a coffee seems
displeasing, and that's life. The lovely
things unpalatable by way of age and circumstance.
Same as pages made of grass and wishes scattered
so the weeds'll grow in thick again this year,
cottonwood piled in the crook where
street meets curb and three hundred
on an A.C. unit for the single hottest
day on calendar.

**Starting at the fifteenth clause of a preamble to a declaration of the liberties of catfish:**

Mention of the bait, sinuous hook dance
current teasing morsel tucked in
murk and sediment, delicious swim
wasting lubricated through the water
like no worm seen yet, must-have once
a rare occasion delicately woven metal
flesh knot twinkling Pleiades at distance,
which is measurable, which closes tail
oscillation quickly looking wet somehow
the closer coming, at which seen clearly
wake of line extends upward through the
pellicle to another place, but which is easily
overlooked as constellation glints spin
porcine nutrient promise slickly through
the mud, close enough to bite, close
enough to swallow, to be momentary
strength slipping palpable down throat
stomach-wise, splitting skin at
gills as seems they always do.

**Revelation verse in six lines:**

Sloppy asphalt gossip through the
A.C. unit vents, gutter drip dreaming.
Better to place confidence in market
fluctuations than in weather forecasts,
than in summer's light-switch ending
coming late this year. Fucking cellphone.

**Neighborhood in several lines,**

but it's midnight and two-stroke juveniles
sound-tunnel their hasty identity issues in
throttle twists my bedroom-wise. Funny, the
indelicate nostalgic thoughts in my maturity,
of signs of impact and of muscle memory.

## Interpretation of a modern ideology

Studied approaches to imperialism
of a certain sense the likes of which
a middle class can get behind,
such affordable leisure and all for
the token risk of storms with people
names and a diffuse sense of racist
guilt another mai thai renders memory,
which, deliberately made curt, is found
to be the way of birds these days, so few
pretty sounds and such difficulty catching.
Consider resource allocation wars
and petabyte identity politicking,
votes for produce managers with
knuckle tats and senatorial campaign
branding contests. Something different
nonetheless, something transcontinental
and easy on the immigration so the
workforce isn't tapped. Lovely sentence,
that, the one with foreign agriculture
ending punctuation easy like inspection
stops and grades on sliding scales
for coffee and cacao; not too
bitter please, the iron rounds its
flavor well already. Trade electrons for
hydrocarbons so the air pollution travels
ear-wise, and the sound of what I want
won't be so deafening as long as it's
at thirty thousand pretty quickly. To speak
of pretty plaster holes plucked in
the wall where a degree had been,
but it was needed for the summer just
to keep the rolling trend.

**Don't Reflect a Lot**

There was a tornado in Vancouver today, which used to be an odd occurrence but which has grown at least modestly common of late. The way things change, I suppose. Tomorrow I put gas into my car and take the freeway for a five-mile trip in traffic to an office of electric servers spinning information up in bytes, typically financial analytics and some research stats. I am an editor, happily deleting words that came about naturally from emails and marketing copy for sake of affect and efficiency. Keep it curt, I tell myself. Don't give them much to second guess. I understand the best way to sell is to build trust, which done with deliberate intent seems itself an exercise in breaking it, but that's just my ethic speaking. Curious. Going to try again tomorrow to deliver a particular image of myself and hope to dodge another twister.

## Catechisms for a Different Day

One night the question lingered
where the moon had first touched
grass, the ocean light salty on its
blades and in the soil something
of a premise or proposal, which
in the circumstance was not
unwarranted but as well did not
presuppose that there were answers.
It was a randomness, the way a sky
might look to those who hadn't spoken
with the wolves at night, a scatter plot
of seconds of a lifetime sorted by
the sounds of birds and the wisdom
of one's mother in the moment
it was catalogued. A greenness.
Must the change come from a
certain lack of pines across the forest
floor? When the wood is flooded with
a silence only heard by others, a
mystery is proposed and it rests
in the soft hands of sunlight on the
other side that one can't see. Which
is to say the answers are yesterday
and tomorrow, the song of a finch
on the telephone wire who preens
a conversation from the cable
as it sings, which, like most things
means so much that it means
nothing.

**William Erickson** studied English and digital arts at Washington State University after many years in the trades. His poetry can be found in *BlazeVOX Journal, GASHER, Cleaver, The Adirondack Review*, and numerous other pubs. William lives in the Portland, OR, area with his wife and two rescue dogs.